THE SHELL H⬤USE

Scottish Contemporary Poets Series
Other volumes in this series include:

Jenni Daiches, *Mediterranean*
Valerie Gillies, *The Ringing Rock*
Kenneth C Steven, *The Missing Days*

THE SHELL HUSE

Gerry Cambridge

Gerry Cambridge

SCOTTISH CONTEMPORARY POETS SERIES

SCOTTISH CULTURAL PRESS

First published 1995
by Scottish Cultural Press
PO Box 106, Aberdeen AB9 8ZE
Tel: 01224 583777
Fax: 01224 575337

© Gerry Cambridge 1995

British Library Cataloguing in Publication Data
A catalogue record for this book is available from the British Library

ISBN: 1 898218 34 X

The publisher acknowledges subsidy from the Scottish Arts Council
towards the publication of this volume

Printed and bound by
BPC-AUP Aberdeen Ltd, Aberdeen

Contents

Gerry Cambridge was born of Irish parents in 1959, and has lived for almost 25 years in rural Ayrshire. In his twenties he worked as a freelance journalist and photographer, specialising in natural history, for magazines such as *Reader's Digest* and *BBC Wildlife*. He now has a particular interest in small press publishing, and is the founder and editor of *The Dark Horse,* an international poetry review with a lively interest in metrical, rhymed poetry. *The Shell House* is his first collection.

Acknowledgements

The author wishes to thank the editors of the following publications, in which some of these poems first appeared:

Acumen, Chapman, Lines Review, New Writing Scotland 12, Northlight, Northwords, Orbis, Outposts, Pennine Platform, Poetry Ireland Review, Poetry Wales, The Spectator.

The author also wishes to record grateful thanks to the Literature Committee of the Scottish Arts Council, for its award of a Writer's Bursary to him in 1994.

Introduction

Gerry Cambridge is more than a promising younger poet; he seems to me to have achieved remarkable things in his verse already. First, he has kept the gate open to the green and blue world of nature that is so bleakly and coldly threatened nowadays. In this age of thickening technology the wonder of stars, clouds, sun, flowers, roots, and waves is quick in him. There is hope for humanity as long as those gates are untroubled.

There is a cosmic element in his verse that is strange, powerful, and moving. The school children emerging from their little prison into a wild burst of sunlight, the behaviour of the clouds in a North Atlantic island as evening draws on, and under the great sweep of the sky a group of islanders sing gospel songs – these are mysterious and marvellous things. He has caught marvellously too the power and rough grace of the earth-worker, and he does it without any condescension of the intellectual or the artist.

He achieves this without having to resort to the anarchic or, more likely, incompetent techniques of much modern verse. He has respect for the traditions, and that is another way of keeping a gate open to what the past has to give us.

There is a great tenderness and warmth in this poetry, towards men, women, and the animals and plants.

Poetry is a hoard of delight against time's ruinings. We must welcome a man who has come to add his talent to the treasury.

George Mackay Brown
Stromness
Orkney

EYE

I am a woman lifting the hem of her dress:
It is the whole Universe loves me.
In it floods, with exquisite lightness.

I am a net of a boat trawling the sea
Of light and I capture the shining shoals
Released by the cosmic jailer, with his key.

The bat's clicking world and the mole's
Beamless kingdom under the Earth
I close on, up here among the jostling souls,

Below that light in the sky that meant my birth
Through the ordinary riddle of days;
Light that made lack of me a dearth.

I yield to the atoms of air a final praise.
By what curious art do they stream in,
Weightless, on the journeying rays,

Through I down here and my blue-flecked twin,
Each of us set on a throne of bone;
By what bright science does the world come in?

The orchard of days will plentifully loan
I, of water, the apples that no teeth bite,
And that never wither, nor any own.

And I'm the happy man's death-held delight;
Composer of airy music, and what must close
On the earth-turned world of sight

Which is all it knows;
A gate, a little well for seas of light,
And that sometimes cannot be filled, or overflows.

ON A HILLTOP

I paint the kitchen doors fresh cherry red
This autumn day, leaving the mind's concerns;
Unconstrained, the mind emptily burns,
So today I love this, sweetly-limited,
Let painting with a wet-bright brush empty my head,
As sunlight enters; and Earth hugely turns
This room, far cities, forests, golden ferns,
That mock with sheer reality the most that's said.
And when I step outside the amazing light
Ignites the miles of gold-frail and earth-strong
Woods to brilliance on the clouds' black-bright;
And the mind dances to reality's song,
As all the miles eastward charge the sight.
Listen if you dare, but never long!

Cunninghamhead Estate

WHISPERS OF TROY

The rifle-shot out in the quiet country dark
Stopped the scratch of my pen on the page.
1 a.m. And then the sound of someone walking,
Scuffling tarmac out there in the lane,
So at the thought of an ordinary rage
My heart beat fast, and nape-hair stood.
Too open, my sitting at a dark uncurtained pane:
Should I go out? I stayed inside
And waited. Whatever was out there
Would be used to the dark like field and wood;
In this known light I half-thought I could hide.
Another shot cracked; this time, part from shame,
And part because it was easier not to wait
For it to come and search me out and thus
Have the advantage of surprise, I peeped
Out of the door; my light-adapted eyes
Saw nothing, but my mind expected the calamitous
Onrush of night's tonnage, like a sudden diesel train
Roaring out of a tunnel. But nothing happened, save
My widening pupils started admitting dark,
And shapes became distinguishable; a figure stood
Out in the lane – then spoke: ''ear that mate?'
Relief: my neighbour. 'Yes, yes; what was it?'
'Foirwurks, oi reckon. Sumwun wi' bleedin' foirwurks.
Bluddy woke me up they did, an' awl.'

I joined him and we went to see
Whatever, though I let him go first
Because he seemed much surer there than me.
The miles of darkness sprawled around;
A quarter moon stood out in the West;
The distant townlights sprinkled the horizon
Like embers or like stars; and there was a torch
Erratic, dancing ahead in darkness, someone out
Already; we heard the tiny voices murmuring
Under the whole star-pinnacled night:
It was two neighbours whom by day I would pass, nodding,
But who in doubt were instantly familiar.
We poked about in darkness near a yew
But never found a thing except for one

Still-burning nearby window light
Belonging to a workman here for months,
A stranger none had got round to knowing.

'Y'd think 'e'd a bin bleedin' aht,' one said,
'After awl them bangs. That bastard's to be kept
An eye on. We don't want games like that
Up 'ere of all the places.' Each agreed:
Grouped thus on one especial night in time
(As was the night they took the city, long ago),
As that gay partial moon, rich yellow,
Stood silently beyond the woods out West,
And all the sound was the river's valley sound;
Nothing else was happening, would happen;
And we stood calmer in that air,
Still touched there by a common glow
That yet was not enough for all to steal
Off into the miles of night for good.

Goodnight; goodnight; goodnight; goodnight.

Thus murmuring, we went our fated ways.

Wide, fabulous night! Dark, supernatural real!

Cunninghamhead

REDWINGS

For that two miles on the unlit road, I loved
(Having left the glare of the village lights)
Passing through the dark-treed countryside
With the star-arrangements above. It was Jupiter

White, and the Pleiades huddled
Above a dark copse on a hill to the right,
And the notes from the first redwings
Back from the North for our winter,
Somewhere up there in the frosty air,
With, ahead and around to horizons,
Dog-barks
Tiny yet definite under those stars.

I stood. Through black fantastical boughs above
Troubled a gust, then all again was still.
Yes, half-putting doubts into words,
An old antiphony,
I stood in the cold,
Hearing the ring of dogs
And the sweet, high, reminders
Of the night-delighting birds.

Cunninghamhead Sonnets

In the early seventies, in my teens, I worked for a local Ayrshire farmer.
These poems, from a longer sequence, record some of those experiences.

I

THOUGHTS ON PASSING A FARM AT NIGHT

A decade gone from Middleton, Davie Smith.
Folk I don't know live there. In winter nights,
Passing, I see them in the kitchen light's
Homeliness – and Davie steps from his small myth
Large into that room. I ate in there, days he'd lie
Napping, in the break from thinning neeps with hoes
Or hands, moving like a tide, up, down, field rows.
The face-spread *Herald* fluttered with his each sigh.

D'ye ken the deefrence, Jimmuck, atween
A bull an' a coo? And while Jimmuck quailed,
Red in his wee free childhood, before he failed:
A bull has a ring in its nose.
                                He was 'green'
Although not after a fashion. As well he's dead,
And commuters live near his sold fields instead.

II

FIELD DAYS

Old Davie still did much farm work by hand.
Tae thin neeps, ye gae up an doon thae rowse.
Leave jist yin each six inches, sae it growse.
The thought of lunch was a breeze-fanned island,
What is the time? our common famous question.
The shrinking patch of field still to be weeded
was joy *and* thought we'd be no longer needed.
He'd blow through his lips: *Gerad, ye're the best yin*
O thae young uns that come here!
                              Or biggest fool
I sometimes thought, those languid days
After the last exams, when I skipped school.

But no jam pieces nor hot tea's tasted more
Significant than that field's, and strongest praise
The two green pounds each day's end, my limbs sore.

III

TAM LUSK

What struck you first of Tam Lusk was his build.
Hot days in the parched fields he'd doff his top,
And adolescent, I could hardly stop
Admiring the minute dance of muscles. Skilled
At labouring, he'd speed on, bare-backed, by
Me in the sun-cracked rows, and when he stood
Finished, his sculpted shining seemed the greatest good
That, skinny, I could ever attain, or try.

Last time we met – a week before he keeled
Over, on his son – at the brambles, he was brown
As a November beech-leaf, hard-wee-village-frown
Smile-banished. He died in minutes in a field.
Old Davie Smith recounted, with escaped half-glee,
This first death that ever trembled me.

IV

DAVIE SMITH'S SISTERS

Childless, destiny stopped with that strange pair.
The kind one, who served lunch, as her calves jiggled
And sagged over her shoes so youngsters giggled,
And the bull-nosed-*Morris* driver, with strict white hair.
A rich-reeking Saturday morning, as I scraped
The byre out, she breenged in like a feisty sparrow,
Hissed, *naw, like this!,* and shovelled the barrow
Furiously full.
                        Aye, some man's escaped,
Tam Lusk commented drily when I told it.

Shimmering in heat-haze, her sister brought
Tea, hot afternoons, into the field, and we would sit
And eat as swallows mazed, twittering, through our thought.

The last I heard, both sisters died in homes.
Their differing presences grace these poems.

PRAISE OF A CROFTER

You'd shove, unknocking, into the croft on the hill where I sat
    in easy despairing
Over the page's bounded snow, and mutter about the rain-
    soaked hay,
The tatties you brought in your bucket, and how the beasts were
    faring –
Storm-unignorable, sweeping my bland blue heaven of choices
    away

With the one word, *Now*. Old drunkard, stubbly abstraction-
    hater, washer 'Wunce a week',
When you'd strip to a vest that hung there in rags as if you
    were freshly tiger-mauled,
Mocker, your laughter bright as the skies, of the folly of what I
    sought, or seek;
Jim Harcus, Jim Harcus, if forever's a lifetime, the name you
    are forever called,

When I went to the North expecting to praise elementals and
    skies,
There you awaited, wheezing like a steam-train, blunt as a hail
    shower –
And more remarkable soon your gale-blazed cheeks and ship-
    containing blue of your eyes
Than argosies dreamt on the seas in a golden hour;

Exemplar of the actual, of the sense I'd have in my every line,
You, clang-solid, brine-bitter, standing over the West's
    Atlantic, clouds arranged about your head,
Or hunching, tractor-borne, through showers, to mend a fence
    to keep in your beasts with twine,
No sipper at bottles, drinker at the fresh original spring of the
    unread,

Dreader of the kirkyard's harbour, you hoarded in boxes and
        letters a life, served up dire home-brew;
Island Apemantus, godless religious man, digger of friends'
        deep graves,
Funeral attender out in unboundaried air on your tractor, beside
        the expansive blue
Drowning the sight of the eye, the final resolving brine that
        dooms and saves,

Thank you, for the many a dark-encircled night we sat up late;
No case of liking you or not: simply there, in your wire-twist-
        buttoned coat;
Reliable as tatties in your bucket, and strong as an iron gate;
Perching the bird of the real in my mind – and anchor, for the
        spirit's boat.

WOMAN ON A PROMONTORY

for Christine Crawford

Here she journeys, gathering flowers.
Atlantic breezes distress her hair,
A far star lengthens her gliding shadow.
And out beyond her, there
To the wide horizon of cobalt sea
A distant red ship's sailing, slowly,
Under the tall white clouds.
And I would wish the woman
Not too attached to flowers,
But let that red ship on her eyes
Whenever she turns to gaze to eastwards
Make sweet, but not too sweet, these amber hours.

11th April, 1990

SKY-CIRCUS

All day the sky-circus passed quickly this window,
At intervals led by the dark ring-masters,
Who set the trees down here panicking, roaring,
And who dropped the snow-whirls from their boots and hair;
They were followed by cronies, bright-black, carrying
         rainbows,
Then ah, groups of elephants, and startle-white stallions –
Such patterns of upblown manes, such plumes –
Some closer, some further, on the plain of the air,
Watched by the lightly-laughing blue-dressed girls....

What a thing was this show from my kitchen door, and I
Surrounded by intimate walls!
Kettle, table, books, and the sink here,
There the processionals dizzily-clear!
Forgive me that seeing I couldn't ignore it,

For I barely settled, as they passed, the whole day –
And already are far down the long sky-road –
Elephants, stallions, rainbows, and blue-dressed girls,
Troupe on troupe, dazzling, bright-black led,
Which opened the soul to such insatiate vistas
It was almost relief when night came, like a saviour, last!

'I'M GOING TO BUY NO APPLES'
overheard

I'm going to buy no-apples,
And I will use no-money,
Handing it to no-girls
In the no-town's shops;

I'll have no-feet in that no-world;
I'll feel no-heat from the no-sun there;
I'll walk among no-people;
I'll breathe in deep the no-air;

So give me a kiss goodbye, my dear,
For O I cannot stay: and soon as I
Step out this door, I'm gone
Forever, into the vast no-day!

DIMINUTIVE

Today where a white house, years back, stood,
The spruces sigh seas above my head;
Now the house has gone, perhaps for good,
The trees tell all its occupants said.

And when I first looked twenty years ago
The tops of those spruces scratch-kissed my knee;
But since, of the two most obvious ways to grow,
I've grown down, or up has grown each tree.

I tilt my head this summer afternoon; mouse-small,
Gaze up at their dark conferring in the breeze,
As the lordly sun above them lounges in his blue hall;
There is but one who among them sees

How their group stands still at my old knee height:
I'm not the giant I used to be, somehow,
Whose high dark head then barred blind light
From such as stand to me like giants now.

THE SHELL HOUSE

When I was younger and the world wide, I sought
The fabulous bird that was over each next skyline;
Here, there, near, far, for twenty empty years
Ignored each simple linnet's nest to roam
Valley and hilltop on a timeless quest;
And came at last to a linnet's clutch,
Five eggs speckled in the lined cup,
And held one up to space; admitting the light,
Frail, the white shell glowed, vessel for earthly gold;
And so I reached the first, last, place,
And distant-travelled rays their dazzling home.

GOLDFINCH IN SPRING

That finch which sings above my head,
Last year's speckled egg, is now
A partner in some nest instead,
That finch which sings above my head,
Buff-gold dandy masked with red,
And hen on eggs upon some swaying bough
That finch which sings. Above my head
Last year's speckled egg is now.

ONCE IN *THE BURKE AND HARE*

Yes, I grew flame-faced there, I'll admit,
When she emerged, black lurex-clad, to dance:
Jerking her pelvis, under the strobe-light.
Too open for me to comfortably sit:
Unlike the leering easy dozens 'round
I couldn't enter the compliant trance,
Nor leave at once, half-liking the sight,
Half-liking the music's mad heart-pound;
Though I soon left, emerged to city sky's
Sun, above black spires. Poor, bleakened Circe,
Not your dance nor gracious flesh offends me,
Nor the dark warm heaven between your thighs.
I may deny no need the wild sun lends me,
But no rich oleaginous man will pocket my eyes.

Edinburgh

MILLIONS WOULDN'T

I sense you're sad when I say, 'Let's be friends,
Not more'; as I am sad, when you agree;
Yet both relieved also, imagining
Now we needn't hide our faults, nor ends
Plot. A prospect changed in seconds! And we
Need not test now the merest brush of lips,
The long love-looks, smiles, touching of fingertips,
The whole, riveting, night-enlarging thing.
Just friends. Ah absolutely. This is quite
Beyond a question now. So buried deep
At last, those old sweet-devious plotters, and
Near-shut what we can barely understand,
That sea-disclosing door ajar of 'might'.
But ah, heaven help us if we peep.

THE STARS OF AUTUMN

We stood below the stars of autumn, and
Whispering with me you proved you knew
That they, also, die. I touched your hand.
We stood below the stars of autumn. And,
Shivering, I tried to say what I had planned,
But did not (though it all came true).
We stood below the stars of autumn, and
Whispering with me, you proved you knew.

ONCE ON THE OVERTOUN ROAD

Beautiful, walking across that high road
In the autumn evening of emerald and blue
And gold; I carried a copy of an old poet's
Late book of country poems, all, now, unfashionable
Lines in my earthly hands illumined
By intimate rays from that star remote
And luminously-silent in the west's hall;
But this was no time
For fashions. Season of ends,
Season for speaking of ultimates,
Of the old desire to be bound forever, good or ill,
To the earth; I felt a journeying
Coolness, already, I saw the world with a new
Clearness, as grasses light-sparkled
Across fields westward, and shadows crept out
Like enemies or like old friends.

ON A SOLITARY WASP THAT NESTED
IN MY KITCHEN

While I've been gone the mother solitary wasp
Has chose a hollow in a piece of wood
Partitioning my kitchen, to celebrate
The whole Creation's motherhood.

She came through the open window meant for post.
All afternoon above my musing head, entering, leaving,
She brings in the outside world, as I write below
Her common path of flight; she's carrying

The bright green grubs as future food
Merely paralysed, to keep them fresh
For the hatching of her blind and hungry young,
A summer off, eager for that flight-enabling flesh;

And flies unerringly up to the hole
For which she has been granted wing,
Alights, and enters it with earthward head,
And heavenward, her vital sting.

Unerringly; though if I stand or change
Position, how it confuses her
Momently, who has this whole internal country
Mapped, and knows me as but furniture.

Soon she reappears from her dark secret place
And goes; a few words later, hovers, laden, back
Before the pane; a buzz announces her
At entry. Who knows how, tiny, she recalls the track

From all out in the wide day where the sun's
Unearthly in the blue, and richly-foliaged trees,
Distance-diminishing, make their sea-sound across
The curving Earth, are glittered and animated by the breeze.

Who knows what lead her surely here
At first, through the open window so to find
Of all the grand world's places possible
The tiny crack thought fitting by her mind;

And raised my murderous choice, to close,
Or let her follow still this season's laws,
And, from the oblivious sun out there
To come, grasping each naked grub between her jaws.

FOXGLOVES

From within the unplumbable dark wood foxgloves came
And quietly assumed that length of ground
Where vegetables till then had greened the sight:
Thus the extravagant wild usurped the tame.
And whether the owner to let them stay
Was weak or strong, no other foxgloves 'round
To grant them ready licence, I can't say;
But from every tight rosette a prospecting stalk
Was updrawn into worldly air by far star-fires,
Then on new-trusting eyes was a sudden gorgeous array
Reflected, a marriage, purple-red and perfect white,
Of windshaken, jostling, congregated spires.
And for one they put an end to ordinary talk,
They reminded of something without a name
That he sought and seems to yet, though years ago
They cast their seed, to colour further air.
If they were torches to light those woods they're out;
In the patch they took, now nettles grow.

WORLDS

From this hilltop I can see the coastal town
This frosty night, its lights like stars or embers
Huddled; and think of the various pubs there,
As in a warm dream within, each laugh, smile, frown:
Tiny-enormous happenings in that comfortable air,
Music, gesture, a mortgage lost or gained, a joke;
An old man muttering of what no one remembers;
Two lovers kissing in the scarves of smoke.
In lengthier conversation, on another scale,
Out here the bright arrangements 'round the sky
Relate among themselves a simpler tale;
And space-backdropped, the soaring pine I walk by
Sways its many limbs with an eerie motion,
A black and star-perched sail, singing of ocean.

NIGHT THOUGHTS

The world is different, two a.m. this winter night:
The gale out of the north has cleared the sky;
Orion, perfect, glitters southwards, high,
Above him Taurus, and at breathtaking height
The Pleiades sparkle in their slow flight
Out in that cold vastness; and all decry
Small ends of earthly effort, wild, as I
Walk here, feeling the chill, an ancient fright;
And the gusty over-dark-trees half-moon there
Though silent makes peculiar music, heard
Apparently not through ears but in the mind,
As out in this tall cavern of the air
The placeless thoughts that come make day absurd,
And all the more a fence to stand behind.

ENCOUNTER WITH A GOD

I met him in the lane, and he was drunk.
Bulbous-nosed, his face a messy sunset:
Crimson, purple, fissured red, streaked wet
By smirr above us in the winter day.
Sixty years of eating, drinking, unable lust:
The bulging ship of the body almost sunk
(And better sunk, many now would say!)
Though the wheezing engine rooms still laboured, just.
Beside him, I felt moderation's epitome,
Who deepen towards the sunset stage of face,
And bodily list already by slow degrees.
Future friend, you'd think we sought spectacular disgrace,
Propriety's end, and truth's final home.
You'd think there was a pearl in those deep seas.

NOVEMBER 19th, 1989

Dreghorn

That afternoon against the black-bright cloud
The world was startle-lit by sudden rays;
As my bus entered the village's one street
The primary children, long-shadowed and loud,
Flooded from the school's wide-narrow gates:
Their faces bright, as if from a furnace blaze
Reflecting, as their little earthly feet
Carried them on to the far, the various fates.
That day, though, they returned to local teas.
Dozens, wild, skipped, shouted, laughed, screamed;
Dragged a heavy satchel, one boy there;
Defeated clips, one little girl's gold hair;
Silent light! Loud children! – a vision seemed
When the old sun threw his far door open, these.

GREAT AND SMALL

Cables like fence-wires strung on sky
And hanging near-taut from arms of giants
Suddenly gleaming in this green place
If crying worked, might make you cry.

They caused a dozen unwept deaths,
The crackling and irreversible fall
(One for every month of the year)
Of trees whose fault was growing tall.

If it's the fault to reach such size
That it would seem to be, for scrub,
Diminutive enough, was spared,
As if such smallness was most wise.

I'd never have thought that such was so!
But then I watched near-helpless men
Crowd-charged, cut the beeches down
That cannot help the height to which they grow.

And now, here, an innocent might miss
What appears to me disease.
An innocent might not guess
That twelve stiff pylons were once trees.

APPLES

for Sam Gilliland

A friend tells me, as a poor child, how he would come
To the apple trees growing where my room is now,
And steal those reddened worlds, heavy in bunches
      On each rough bough,
And magically made from light, from earth, from air;
      And some
Would have grown perhaps in this very spot
Where many a stormy winter night, I sit in this armchair

Writing. A distance of forty-five years between!
The orchards cut down, the extent of his journey,
And how that bright outside would be now within, my friend
      Couldn't foresee;
Who has come to the grey-haired man from the child
      Unseen
But not undone, for changed to the man, it's said.
Still, though, I believe he's back there, running wild,

A small figure, down the estate lane, then
Off under restless beeches and down the Overtoun Road,
And over the hill under sun and clouds at Warwickdale
      With his borrowed load;
Existing forever in that place, and in that time;
      And my pen
Glides and weaves across the page tonight
As if it followed him, and his sweet crime.

Cunninghamhead Estate

LODGER

To the mewing at my kitchen door
I open up and let come in
From a night of showers and wind-roar
The old familiar one
At a late-early hour.
Whiskers, wild dark eyes, and purr!
O she is mad with affection
As the caught stars of Atlantic droplets glint
In the night earth-heaven of black fur;
And now is a good weight in my arms,
A damp paw on my neck's hot skin:
Vision of random otherness comes,
And it complements this glare within;
So something in me gently yields
As I am touched by this untouched,
And printed by wide night-fields.

LITTLE DRAMA

A bonny night. I step outside and gaze,
Head back in autumn dark, up into space,
Where stars between the clouds burn with quiet praise,
And think for whatever reason of your face.

Fine thoughts below those glittering Pleiades.
Regrets. Goodbyes. The largeness of the night
Summons easy nostalgia for futilities,
Free from the searching glare of window light.

But what's this, suddenly, about my feet,
Rubbing at my ankles? It's the old, fat black tom
Unusually affectionate, startling from
Revery, ragged-eared, with his small thunder.
Is it mere food, or love he wants, I wonder?
His presence somehow makes the night complete.

IN JANUARY

A promised good is appreciated most:
And that is why this beam –
(Entering as it always does
This month, my kitchen window),
Celestial magician
Making of this pane a door,
Charging to bright pale gold
The crumbs of the breakfast toast,
Marrying, far-travelled,
In brilliance this white page –
Delights me, I think, more
Than it will do again, and did, before,
In the blander
Summers of its taller age.

For here the wood is all uncarved yet,
And here the canvas is untouched;
Still to be written the marvellous verses,
Unuttered yet frustration's curses,
And undenied by actual hillocks
The inner ranges, cherished, we must hide!

JOSEPH'S VISITANT

The black cat, not even mine,
Still spends days and days in here.

A monstrous tom with great muscular haunches,
Five hidden hooks
On each white mittened paw,
And a bib
Clean as a summer cloud.

As he lolled this morning on his side on the couch
Like an emperor, like a plump Nero,
Fastidiously licking the sole of his right forepaw,
After a while I could resist no longer
And to annoy him gently threw
A packet of staples, a propelling pencil, a red biro,
While he mused on as each
Flew through the air towards him.
With slitted eyes and long regimental whiskers
He followed those parabolas
With moving head, like a tennis match spectator's,
The look on his chops enigmatic
As some replete guru's.

Then when he slept, later, I
Ruffled his shining fur. He
Lay there unconscious. But soon there came
A low moaning deep in his throat,
His head lifted a little,
His breath came short and harsh,
And he turned round and the eyes
Slowly and gently opened a fraction
To show the fierce green and the dark pupil.

Just now when the neighbour's kitten
Peeped through the open door, I brought her in,
Carried her where
The black cat lay on the couch behind a cushion, staring out.
The little one hissed at the giant.
The giant was unconcerned.

Ah, but the fascination he exerted!
When I put the kitten down on the carpet
She lounged a moment below my typing stool.
She whisked her tail, bemused.
Then set off across the carpet, sniffing,
Tail at the tip just trembling, the whole of her
Tense as a child listening
For the least crack as she crossed thin ice.

She stopped at the couch and backed away,
Leapt to my lap for succour, flowed as honey
Onto the carpet, sprang from there
To a chair where my white papers lay,
Shamrocked them with faint mud,
And stood, with her forepaws up on the arm-rest,
Peering. Her whiskers tinily-stirred.
What to do about the thing behind the cushion?
It wouldn't go away, it was always there.

At six years old I stood at the rail of a ferry
With a half-crown in my hand, a fortune to me.
How I was tempted to drop that coin,
See it fall irretrievable into the waves, a loss
Disastrous, deep down there in the black!
I would open a little my small moist hand.
The coin would have settled in mud down there, heavened
By fish and boats and clouds and constellations.
Nothing on Earth could have brought it back.

And sitting on top of *Clo Kervaig* with you,
I had to say, 'Imagine falling! Imagine I walked
Just to the edge, to stare over, and slipped?
I would be there at the edge, then not there,
Quite irretrievably gone. What would you do?'
We sat four hundred feet
Above the waves in the white sun
Where fulmars flew like believable angels
And wind frayed our hair. 'Laugh,' you said, 'probably, at
       first.'

The black cat sleeps on my couch now, in the afternoon.
He was out all night, smells faintly of silage.
I may not resist the unsprung traps of his paws.
I may just tweak his tail a little, to bubble his cauldrony blood.

And you, kitten, I will put you out now.
You have had enough of such temptation.
You and I
Who fear and delight in the same thing, perhaps.

Note: Clo Kervaig is a sea-cliff near Cape Wrath, Sutherland.

GAIA

Out of the forge
Of root, flower, rock –
Voice, gesture, look.
Here is a touching
Hand, warm
As a sunlit
Stone; and this,
It might have been
Anything, yet
In such shape
It came: mire
That stands
Beside me; miracle
Of assembled
Atoms that grows
Old, balancing life
On breath's
Fulcrum, accompanying me
In the light
Of a yellow star.

LAST LINE

Among long-shadowed dykes
And the dabbed tints of flowery ditches,
He was a distant gleam on a penny-
Whistle along the lane
In the lemon evening light,

A shivering brilliant song
By fingers danced from breath's
Essential quietude: alchemy, like raindrops
Lit by a sudden beam! Sea's molten pewter made
Vast susurrations in the ears'

Caverns as he came
Onwards without stopping, no, nor even slowing so
He seemed to step
Every second afresh through
The marvellous flare of making. Happiness

None had told him was impossible. Found,
He played alone. Indoors the islanders
Glowed on their faces Africa. Wave
After wave of shooting crashed in their ears.
That storm the piper's small notes drowned.

Papa Westray, 1985

NORTH

The jewel-lit noon of the bombing,
  In a sparse land of stone
I walk the dazzling shore
  To Faraid Head, alone.

Mountains sleep on the skyline
  In the silver and emerald day,
And there's the target island,
  Tiny, miles across the bay.

I leave the shore: a short cut
  Through silent dunes and grass,
To reach the closest vantage,
  And watch all that may pass:

When over my head, three jets streak –
  Silence, then a roar.
The horizon's hidden here,
  By hillocks all before.

So I run, run, run up one –
  There's the island suddenly
And the first jet shrinking over it
  On a white cloud, darkly.

I raise binoculars tremblingly:
  Poise in a black-ringed bubble of light
The island screed from earlier bombs,
  The target hut on its extreme right...

And see in the bubble how delicately
  The jet-loosed bomb twirls down,
Like a tiny seed that, spinning,
  Mirror-flashes to the sun.

And glittering down through deep air –
  It kisses the island, flashes –
Silent, orange on white and blue
  Outblossoms an instant, vanishes.

I lower binoculars tremblingly:
  Unchanged the island sits there still,
Smoke-columned now in brilliant air,
  As I here, on my small hill

Listen long for the shock –
  As clouds like bubble-pearls stand round,
As the smoke rises, wisping –
  For the bomb has made no sound.

Yes, listen in eerie silence here,
  And with a feigned desire
Think this less than it appears,
  Merely a silent fire.

Think it less as seconds tick
  And over the miles of water
News now glides of a cataclysm
  Not meant for slaughter –

Then the tight orgasmic bang.
  As if the sky should crack, fall,
And mountains, crofts, blow away,
  Though all stands just as usual –

Except Earth jolts, as if a giant
  Jumped to ground, off the sun;
Yelping gulls upflurry like snow,
  A flock of far sheep run;

And horizons to sharpness tremble back
  As the second jet roars in,
Like a thought catapulted over the island,
  And each wing like a fin.

And six dream-times all happens
  As massive Earth turns, slow:
Flash – calm – bang-rocked shining world –
  Till the jets, in seconds, go.

And dazzle spreads over the wrinkled sea
  As an oystercatcher, nesting, calls;
As in a waiting amphitheatre,
  Breeze-ruffled silence falls.

Faraid Head, Durness, Sutherland, 1986

Note: R.A.F. target bombing of An-garbh-eilean (stony island) off Cape Wrath, can be watched from the nearby headland of Faraid Head. All details in the poem are documentary.

WINTER THOUGHT

From an old outbuilding up on a hill
Near a croft overlooking the grey, white-flecked Atlantic
That's visible now through slant-sleet squalls,
John MacLeod pulls out the bales
To get his beasts through the winter
I helped him to store there, under the sun;

The sea was a cobalt limitless plain
With far small clouds, blossoming, slow,
And a destroyer lavish with guns
Which, sitting down in the bay to begin,
From the first to the final load of hay
Diminished into the afternoon, and dropped
From sight as the sun moved round.

So John MacLeod pulls the bales out
Of which the last put in are the first removed;
And so, too, in the mind's sleet-storm
I hope will not continue long,
I, also, struggle, to pull out the golden bales
Packed with the eastern horizon, and its calm clouds,
And that one grey ship there,
Stored when the day was warm.

ISLANDER

The old man sat all day in the chair in that island room.
Through the one pane
That gave on Atlantic clear to Canada, tankers and merchant
       vessels
Grew tiny, tiny, and dropped off over the edge of the world,
And the sun went down there, most days, summers,
Touching the walls in the room with its light like a song.

The old man sat all day.
Occasionally
He would make an expedition to the back park,
A field that sloped to the shore, where I met him first
In resonant island air. (Hair-wisps, cloud-wisps,
Faint tiny cumuli grouped in the west
And the vessels broken in his cheeks by the long slow storms of
       nights and days.)
We spoke, leaning on the opposite
Sides of a dry-stane dyke, our voices punctuated
In the silence by shrieks from the light-crazed cities of nesting
       terns
As a ship
Minute on the west's grey plain
Sailed for the orange blaze that the hid sun stained.

Thereafter
Waved to by his wife at the far croft door
I'd visit in passing, to see him.
His occasional leading questions
Were, to my loud earnestness,
Doors ajar, glimpses of gaiety
In some of the rooms unlocked in his head
As, in the silence, the clock's tick
Went on notating
The beats of our hearts and the passage of ships round the
       islands.

One morning he went out, I heard, to the byre
And never came back. Isabel found him, he who had sailed
In the Second World War, nor spoke of it,
Whose words to me
Were like the feathered corks of the eiders, down in the
            turbulent bay,
Or like the ships framed in the window
Inching calmly and carefully
To the port of the sunk sun over the unfathoming deeps.

Orkney

THE DRUNKEN LYRICIST

We met that grey dull evening on the east shore.
Roaring round the bend he came, flat out
at fifteen miles an hour, and stopped. We had to shout
till he turned off his engine. *It's going to pour*
it looks like: me. *Oa, I'm haardly cancerned*
thee night wi weather, man! he said, flat cap askew.
Gap-toothed smile. Torched cheeks. Eyes' Atlantic blue.
Hiv you seen any? Weemun? Whisky burned
its golden road in him, and he would search.
's that wun, man? – the shore's dark speck.
Not waiting a reply, through the bright wreck
of that grey evening, he roared off, with a lurch.
His tractor almost reared on its back tyres.
Fifteen miles an hour flat out, parched by amber fires.

SKY SONG

The sky seemed truer than the God in the book,
That dusk of the outdoor service on Orkney;
It was a carnival, constantly-changing: the colours
Slate-grey, blue-grey, rich berry-purple, magenta,
With startle-white clouds like tall brides among them, near, far,
    over the sea
That westward curved clear to America. And we stood on the
    earth
With the silent congregation, the lichen-bewhiskered and
    sullen-faced,
Black, red, pink-veined, drunkenly-leaning stones,
While at our hands a wind from immensity attempted riffling
    the pages –
Searching, searching – of the hymnals we sang from
Morning has Broken, in discordant voices, accompanied by an
    old lady
Playing an accordian badly, yet with such a lack of despair that
    I nearly laughed:
Ah, the rich farce of the Human! (When I was young, I looked
    up to adults.)
And miles to westward when I raised my eyes
To where the lit blue of the sky was radiant,
Over far Westray, huge-tiny cumuli, long and humming
Choirs of cumuli, deepened to rose on their tops in the last of
    the light,
And I tilted my head there to clouds high as mountains,
Shining with light as if tipped with snow,
That reddened in turn; and looking back round
At the circle of singing, intimate faces, saw they were
    sky-glowed,
The minister's white hair a lambent rose in the gloom,
Hair that the wind raised, indicating heaven –
All of us there in our circle stained
Magenta and rose by immense sky-events, up among the passes
    of the clouds;
But already the rosepearl light in the cumuli westward
Was fading perceptibly, followed by that in the clouds
    above us:
The musician of day, playing his flute,
Walking away down the lonely sky-road

Off into silent distance, as we stopped our singing, and service
  over,
Handed out tea and biscuits, our cold hands ringing the hot
  cups;
Our tiny figures near the wall of the church
Shivering, as the wide sky altered silently: the musician of the
  heavens
Striding off, and the clouds
Fading and fading as a great thing left them –
Those far beyond the lighthouse on Westray, those to the South,
And those high over small heads there, passing through chord
  on chord to silent grey.

*Note: Outdoor services were held for a time beside a ruined church on
Orkney. The services were intended to help with fundraising activities to
have the church repaired. Repairs were completed in 1994.*

AMBITION

On a wide northern shore
 I found a house of stone
Cold in island silence;
 And lived alone

Below the sun
 With seabird cries,
And other things
 Without disguise.

Likely that is why,
 Since then,
I try persuading blindness
 Back, to see again.

AN OLD CROFTER SPEAKS

Oa, cum an in an' doan't stand at thee doar!
I doan't get meny cum ti see me noo.
Here, sit thee doon. Ah, that must be where
Wun o' me cats browt in a rabbit, luk,
Last night. I try ti stap them doin' it,
But that's chust hoo they're made. Yaas, yaas.
That is chust hoo they're made. As you kin see,
I'm nat much o' a hoosekeeper. Until
Me mither died, in nineteen eighty-two,
She wid tek care o' that fer me, but noo
Thee hoal thing is chust left ti do mesel'.
As weel as which this dwellin's noo so oald
It's finisht aboot wi' dampness, an'
Winniver I hev dun wi' beasts ootside, it's aall
I manidge ti mek me food, an' chust sit here.
I s'poase I shood hee merreed. Ah, but there
Wus nat a single woman here wid tek me.
Why shood that be, man? Nat a single wun.
It may be it wus me oan falt, afore
I understood chust hoo. It aall began
When I wus in me teens. They'd hoald
A dance doon in thee haall each Setterday.
(There wus much moar foak livin' here than noo.)
Me father wus thee fiddler, an' becaas
I wus ashayemd ti dance a front o' him,
I nivver danced at aall, I nivver gat
Over me fear o' dancin', an' sumtimes
I think it aall stems back ti that. Thee weemun,
Why, they were aff wi' aall thee ither men
Who'd dance, y'see, so I wus left mesel'.
Oa, Jean Breckness affert wunce ti tek me,
Six hooses farther Narth, but that wus bek
In nineteen sixty-sevan, when her foaks
Hed died. Bluddy hell, that wus no yoose ti me;
Why, she coodna hev carried chuldren,
She wus chust too oald. Whut yoose wus that ti me?
Oa aye, I went ti her aall right, until
She toald me she'd two ither men, who came
Visitin' on her reggular, and did I meet wun
Anytime? Why, bluddy hell, I thowt

Why wid I waant ti meet wun foar, ti ask
Er ti be toald if she went well thee night?
So I stapped goin' then, y'see, becaas
Thee ither two were merreed, and I thowt
If sumthin' heppened her, I might end up
Hevvin' ti raise a yung un nat me oan.
It wid be moar respectabul if she
Cood point ti me, y'see, a batcheller.
But anyway, we didna waant each ither.
There's nivver been a woman here I'd waant
That aalso waanted me. Oa, o' coorse it wid
Hee made me happy, man. O' coorse it wid.
Ah, but that's dun noo. Oa, I cood hee left
When duzzens o' yung weemun left, when thee
Last waar wus an, an' nat cum bek, but then
Me foaks hed no wun here ti wurk thee craaft,
An' waanted me ti stay. An' so I stayed
Y'see, but aall thee weemun left, an' moast
Nivver came bek at aall. Bluddy hell, an' why
Shood they cum bek ti this hoal o' a place,
This hoal o' a smaall island? Sumtimes I think
That even hed they dun so, it wid nat
Hev changed things in thee least. I s'poase I mean
I've allus been quite shy, an' then thee moar
I liked a woman, why, thee shyer I
Becayem. Hoo do you mek oot that wun?
You're thee intellekchul, man, nat me.
Is that nat chust reedeecullus? You wid hee thowt
Thee apposite shood be thee case, an' yit
It nivver wus wi' me, an' aall becaas
O' bluddy shyness. (This is thee drink
Taalkin' thee night, I s'poase; oa, sumtimes,
I wish I cood hee been drunk aall thee time,
Wi'oot thee bad eeffects, o' coorse, becaas
Thee drink taalks moar than I cood manidge
Ivver.)
         Er we nat hevvin' chust a fine
Time o' it thegither? Ah, but it must end,
It must cum ti an end. Oa, round aboot
Thee sixties there, when I cood wurk oot hoo
Thee hoal thing hed ti end, it gat so bad,
Me depresshan gat so bad, I chust hed
Ti see thee dactor. I felt I cood haardly
Do enythin' at aall, me mind wus chust,

Oa, chust aboot entiyerly seized up. Yaas.
So I hev hed whut you wid caall a moast
Unsuccessful life. Oa, bluddy hell,
I canna see hoo you mek that oot!
Lats an' lats o' foaks seem heppier than me.
Why, when aall they visiturs cum here an' say
'This is a luvlee island', aall I can say's
'It hasna been sae bewtifool ti me.'

That's why I hev ti drink so much, y'see.
Chust drink an' lie here blatto, yaas, chust lie
Here bluddy blatto, on me oan. Cood I
Hev found a woman, I'd nat hev needed that.
Why, even if wun o' they yung wuns, that cums
Visitin' this smaall island, affert me
Her bady, likelee it's too late. Yaas, yaas.
I've lawest me tinkul, I'm chust dun.
No' like you, you've gat a lat left in you yet.
But lissun ti me noo, yoor time is lumutud.
Lum-u-tud. Go ti it man, while you've thee chaance!
You waant ti end up sum oald man like me,
Sum oald drunk man like me? I'll soon be gan,
I'll soon be in me bluddy bax, you'll hev
Ti taalk wi' me up at thee kirkyard, there.
Hoo deep hev they ti dig? Oa, chust deep enough
Ti mek shoor that you'll nat climb oot again.
That needna be too deep, o' coorse, at aall.
Yaas, yaas, I've dug sum mesel'; they ask
Thee friends ti dig thee grave, y'see. Hoo deep?
Oa, wi' thee last wun there, I think I mind
After thee first foot it gat exsepshanally saaft,
So we were doon ti thee roape-ends afore
Anywun realised it; yooshally it's nat
So deep, fer if there bees a lat o' rocks
An' stoanes, sumwun or ither yooshally
Suggests we mek it do. But it may be
We aalso thowt that when his sister dies
She cood be put in o' thee tap o' him,
Ti save moar wurk. That's mebbe whut we thowt,
Fer she'll nat live forivver. Sum jaab that,
Diggin' throo oald bits o' boanes an' teeth –
Fer it's teeth last thee langest. Yaas, yaas.

Oa, bluddy hell, you doan't believe in that!
Manshuns in thee sky! If you think so,
Chump in thee sea tomarrow! Oa, chust go
An' chump inti thee sea! But when I go
Up ti thee hoose on Mundy, you'll be there.
An' tell me why is that? Becaas you know
That no such place exists. It exists here?
You like ti look at clouds? Oa aye.
Cut oot aall that reeleejan stuff wi' me!
Hev I nat toald you that afore? Aall that
Is chust preetenshasness, reeleejan's chust
A pack o' bluddy lies! Ah, but you doan't
Mean it as thee ithers do, o' coorse.

Lissun, man, chust lissun ti me noo.
I mind when me father an' me unkul wus alive.
Me unkul wus a teacher, whut you'd caall
A skallar; when he were yung he nivver hed
His face oot o' a book; he's deid, o' coorse.
Me father went ti see him in thee haspeetal.
His belly wus aall swoallen up, an' he
Lifted bek thee cuvvers so's ti show
Me father hoo it wus; me father wus disgustet.
Me father hed an intrest in astronomy.
He liked ti go oot on a night, an' luk
Away up at thee staars. But anyhoo,
Him an' me unkul, they wid sit sum nights
Away inti thee smaall oors in that hoose
Doon at thee shoar, discussin' aall them things.
It's empty noo; full o' rats an' slaters. Anyhoo,
When I wus smaall I'd lissun. Bluddy hell,
Sumtimes they'd try ti taalk away thee night!
Thee thing aboot it wus it left them no
Wiser than afore. So I thowt I'd
Chust save mesel' thee trubble, an' ferget
Aboot they saarts o' things, so that's thee road
I took an' hev stuck ti.
                              Will you nat stay
An' tek anither pint wi' me at least?
Ah, you hev ti go; it'll be dark be noo.
You hev ti waalk a few miles yet, ti bed.
Me oan bed is chust here. Thanks anyhoo,
Fer visitin'.
                    Will you mind o' these nights?

Will you mind o' these nights when I'm nat here?
We might nat hee been sittin' like this, were
Me father nat thee fiddler. Ah, but I
Wus frightened they wid laff at me, y'see.
I'll allus wish I'd bluddy danced when yung.

1988

craaft – croft
lawest – lost
saaft – soft
saarts – sorts

SOLSTICE

The morning I should have heard R. S. Thomas
Reading his poems in a hot far room,
I woke here in silence to primrose rays
Moment by moment shock-freshly arriving
To steam-wisped kettle and page in the gloom:
Cells of light, a pristine praise.

Spruce were viridian, out on the blue-black,
The world a bright hall, sparse-furnished, austere;
Leaping and lively the cat came in from the myriad ways
Through the bare-treed woods and the fields outspread
And shone in the universe, local here:
Cells of light, a pristine praise.

I lifted a teaspoon, and that had a meaning,
As the voice intoned in a distant place
For the forest of faces, the fortunate phrase:
I wrote on the page from the west to the east
As entered here from the sun in space
Cells of light, a pristine praise.